Boost Your Career Success By Developing Your Soft Skills

SADANAND PUJARI

Published by SADANAND PUJARI, 2024.

Table of Contents

Copyright 1

About 2

Introduction 3

Success Rituals Fundamentals 4

Rituals OF Highly Successful Individuals (Part 1) 8

Rituals OF Highly Successful Individuals (Part 2) 12

Empowering & Disempowering Rituals 19

Building Your Own Success Rituals 23

6 Core Success Rituals 26

Morning Success Rituals 29

Evening Success Rituals 31

Conclusion 35

Copyright

Copyright © 2024 by **SADANAND PUJARI**

All rights reserved. No part of this book may be reproduced, scanned, or distributed in any printed or electronic form without permission. Please do not participate in or encourage piracy of copyrighted materials in violation of the author's rights. Purchase only authorized editions.

Boost Your Career Success By Developing Your Soft Skills

Assess Your Personal Development Skill, Create Your Action Plan To Boost Career Success

First Edition: Jun 2024

Book Design by **SADANAND PUJARI**

About

Double Your Goal Achievement in Half the Time While Working Smarter. What do tennis greats Federer, Nadal, Murray and Djokovic have to do with Personal Productivity, Goal Setting and Achievement? It's all about their EXPERT follow through—they finish their swings and they work SMARTER, not always HARDER!

The way the world is going, personal productivity is becoming more and more important, and I can teach you how to get from point "A" to point "B" with supreme efficiency. They say "it's the busy people that get things done—so, if you want to get things done ask a busy person", but to me busy, is not always efficient or effective. Maybe the saying should go, "ask a productive person"?

In this Book, I help you capture your best ideas with goal setting for every aspect of your life and make them reality. You will gain the confidence to do the IMPORTANT things, and stop being a slave to unproductivity.

The secret sauce? Great goal setting systems to guarantee your follow through, to make things happen, and lead your most PRODUCTIVE life. You're learning what I as a goal setting life coach teaches my clients.

Learn these whip-smart ideas and personal productivity systems and get yourself to the top of your game by working smarter, with these proven winner strategies.

Wake up energized for your day tomorrow—let's get going!

Introduction

You want to become successful. You can feel that there is more to life than what you are presently enduring. It has crossed your mind more than once that maybe you are doing things the wrong way. You need a new approach to ensure you give life your best shot at becoming one of the individuals that history can never forget. You can make your indelible mark on the line of history as a successful person by trying some success rituals. You are right about needing an approach to attain success. Success rituals share insight into steps that successful individuals conduct daily and some that you might want to implement in your life. The natural order of life is that things go through stages. Success rituals are processes that individuals endure to become prosperous achievements during the stages are different for everyone.

However there are similarities in each stage of the success rituals just as there are similarities in the stages to produce a child but the outcome differs. Success rituals have certain fundamentals that every successful individual had to do and some which they had to learn how to overcome. Likewise you must decide without any form of doubt that you two will have to work hard and overcome whatever obstacles you will encounter on your journey. You might be the one that will develop before the expected timeframe for one to become a success. Do not delay for another minute. It is time to discover empowering success rituals which will assist you to conquer your fears and progress on your destined journey of prosperity.

Success Rituals Fundamentals

In this chapter we'll talk about the success rituals fundamentals. So what exactly is ritual? Ritual is just a synonym of the word habit. We all know that our thoughts and actions over a period of time will determine how we progress in life. Positive rituals yield positive results and negative rituals will produce undesirable results. We have so many rags to riches stories and you might be a rags story awaiting the right rituals to change your situation to riches. But did you know that you will never know until you examine your life and make the necessary modifications. It is time to change your perception about rituals.

Have you ever come across individuals with similar success rituals but they all produce different results? This is because everyone has different opportunities and how we react to situations is different. Notably persons will have similar talent but each talent comes with a unique ability. If you do not discover the uniqueness that comes with your talent you might never truly stand out from the others. Better in the exact field as you are if you cannot produce extraordinary results then your advancement will be either mediocre or below average mediocre and below average results will never give you the title of a successful person. You will only discover the uniqueness that comes with your talent.

After you have started using your talent let's take a look at some success rituals fundamentals that you must ensure you develop to build your rock solid success rituals starting with those listed on the ladder below. The first step on the success rituals fundamentals is to believe in you. If you do not believe in yourself you will never really discover your true potential. Apart from finding what hidden treasures of skills you have buried within is knowing how and when you are at your best. Some people will tell you that they think it is better to have a hot cup of coffee after they take a shower or go for a jog than ideas will start to overflow in their head.

Think back to the time you were able to unravel your best idea so take a moment to ask yourself what were you doing at the time that happened. And where were you when that happened. If possible go back to that exact location and repeat the same action of what you were doing and try to discover more great ideas. You'll need to purchase a notebook. It's imperative that you always have something close by to write down your thoughts. I'm suggesting that you get a notebook because ideas will pop in your head at various hours of the day or night. Developing the healthy habit of jotting down your ideas also gives you the opportunity to better analyze your plans and to be able to group or tweak them.

That is progress and you will feel good at what you've accomplished and be more motivated to put them into action. You are elated now because you have chosen what you believe is the best idea and you are ready to put it into action. It will be at this moment that fear will opt to cripple your mind creating doubts about your idea and your ability to implement them successfully. The only way to dispel your fear is to take the necessary steps to set realistic goals and timelines for your concepts. The moment you decide to continue with your ideas you will feel the power fear has over your mind slowly losing its grip. Fear will entirely lose its grip on your mind when your concept becomes an action so go ahead.

Even if you have to move with wobbling legs and shaking fingers Take your leap of faith. Now let's talk about the fundamentals ladder of success rituals: goal setting and time management are equally important on the success rituals fundamentals ladder. If you do not set targets with timelines then you will have nothing to work towards and no achievements to look forward to. Celebrating hard work and determination is what will transform your goals into reality. If you only work hard some of the time then you should anticipate the partial result. A mind that is determined is the fuel for hard work and hard work keeps you determined.

That is why both of them have to be used together consistently. For me the final success ritual's fundamentals is never fear failure. It's inevitable that you will fail at some stage of your plan. Failure varies for different individuals. You might experience a massive failure and you'll have to start your journey entirely from the first step. Your failure might be minor and with a few adjustments things can be back on the progress level. If you fear failure you will not be able to recover from misfortunes.

When you face failure, accept it, analyze what is the possible cause or causes and start strategizing immediately to correct as well as prevent it from recurring your fears will begin to diminish. Success rituals are crucial because we all need them to become successful. Take things step by step while you discover yourself and find your sole purpose for being awarded the gift of life. Learn to enjoy your rollercoaster ride that life is guaranteed to take you on. Remember that no matter how badly you fail you can always rise again. If you work hard and if you are determined enough.

Rituals OF Highly Successful Individuals (Part 1)

In this chapter we'll talk about the rituals of highly successful individuals and how it will help you get ahead of the regular folks in life. Now let's take a look at the morning evening and business rituals of some highly successful individuals. Number one Mark Zuckerberg co-founder and CEO of Facebook. I'm wondering if you noticed that the man who has his name and is listed on almost all the billionaire lists that you can grace your eyes on seems to only have gray t-shirts . These gray t-shirts are not a uniform for his company. The wearing of only gray t-shirts by Mark Zuckerberg is a deliberate act. It's his way of saving time in the mornings even after he is sometimes up all night having a discussion with an employee.

You could still find Mark Zuckerberg up when the clock strikes 6:00 in the morning without having to worry what clothing to wear for the day. Mark Zuckerberg grabs his outfit which is usually his gray T-shirt and then he's off to work at his office early in the morning. No to put Masri warrior CEO next U.S. a true warrior of time and rising early in the mornings to complete most of her tasks is put Masry warrior while the night shadows cover the land and with the twinkling of the stars which probably reminds her that she's among the most successful women at four thirty in the morning Pat Masry warrior is up and working but Masri warrior starts the day by going through her emails for approximately an hour.

Then she ensures she is kept informed about current affairs by reading the newspaper after her reading of the papers. Then it is time to ensure she remains fit and healthy so she exercises after her daily morning rituals. She's in her office by eight thirty in the morning ready to take on the challenges of a new workday. TIM COOK CEO APPLE Tim Cook not only enjoys his race of being up before the sun but he is very proud of the fact that he is the first one to be at his company in the mornings and the last one to leave during the evenings. You can check for an email from Tim Cook as early as forty five in the morning because that's when he gets up and has become known for sending company emails at that time in the mornings. Tim Cook is one who ensures that he maintains his health.

Therefore you can find him in the gym by 5:00 in the morning. Jack Dorsey co-founder Twitter Tweet tweet might be some of the twittering that Jack Dorsey hears at five thirty in the morning when he is taking his six mile jog. Jack Dorsey also takes some time to meditate before he leaves for his run in the mornings Jack Ma founder Ali Baba group as precious and swift as the wind is the commodity time. We cannot preserve time and one's past. We can either give thanks that we have used our time productively or live with the regrets of what we never used our time to accomplish.

Knowing how precious time and his family are, Jack Ma's up by seven in the morning at the latest Jack Ma uses half an hour to complete some task and then he ensures he spends some quality time with his family Karen golden founder and CEO. Hint water it's time to take a hint. Most highly successful individuals are hitting the work button before the day is Dawn and Karen

Golden is among those who are doing so. Karen Golden's day begins at five thirty in the morning. She pursues through her work calendar ensuring that she has no exigent meetings. And then she responds to emails by 715.

Kara golden starts making her business calls but not before she saturates her tastebuds with a double latte and she goes hiking with her husband David Kush CEO VIRGIN America. Crunch time is at 415 in the morning for David Kush. His fingers get busy to dial his associates numbers who are on the East Coast but not before he took some time to send emails. Next David Kush tunes his ears to Dallas sports radio while his eyes are kept busy reading the newspaper then he's off to the gym to ensure he keeps himself fit Dan lead director next desk. It's time for a standing ovation because Danley is up by the clock strike of three thirty in the morning Dan Danley ensures that he is completely hydrated by drinking two liters of water.

Then he also consumes two cups of coffee and smooths things off with a smoothie. After Danley hydrates his body the next 90 minutes he shares with his dog and reading. He reads for one hour and spends half an hour with his dog clearing his paws through perspiration. You can find Danley in the gym from five fifteen to six fifteen in the morning when the clock ticks its way to 715 in the morning. Danley is already in his office prepared to tackle the challenges of a new workday Sally Krawcheck co-founder CEO Elon vest. It is the romancing of the mind with the lights dimmed or sometimes she seeks warmth from the fireplace along with a hot cup of coffee and Sally Krycek is ready to start her day at 4 in the morning while the lights might be dimmed in her home at 4 in the morning.

Sally crawled check a shining bright with ideas because that is when her creative flair comes to light. Best Indra Nooyi CEO PepsiCo popping as early as 4:00 in the morning is Indra Nooyi. Her first task is ensuring that her plans are organized for the new day. Ingenuity is usually buzzing in her office by 7:00 in the morning Richard Branson founder and chairman Virgin Group. He is certainly no virgin when it comes to rising early. Not even the comfort of his private island can prevent him from pulling his curtains at five forty five in the mornings to watch the rising of the sun with a fantastic view of the rising sun which comes with the opportunity to enjoy his fortune for another day. Richard Branson maintains his health by exercising and having a healthy breakfast. Then he's off to work to ensure that he keeps making his billions.

Rituals OF Highly Successful Individuals (Part 2)

Now let's move on to talk about the evening rituals of five highly successful individuals. Number one Bill Gates CEO Microsoft. Bill Gates was dubbed the richest man in the world according to Forbes billionaires list. He reads for an hour almost every night before going to bed no matter how late he gets home. One of the topics that have consistently sustained his reading habit is business related issues which Bill Gates uses to assess changes in the market. No surprise right there. He also reads about politics and health care Joel Gascon CEO buffer walking for 20 minutes every evening during his walk. Joel Gascon assesses his workday and analyzes his greatest challenges. And then he will slowly stop thinking about work when the shadow of tiredness takes over his body.

Arianna Huffington founder Huffington Post at night Arianna Huffington disconnects from the world of technology by turning off all her electronic devices. Then she dissolves the stress from her workday by taking a hot bath. Arianna Huffington pulls the shutters on her day wearing her pajamas while she reads a physical book Kenneth Chennault CEO American Express Kenneth Chennault gets a head start to his day by setting goals for three things he wants to achieve every night before he goes to bed Oprah Winfrey businesswoman and media mogul Oprah Winfrey ends her days. Just how she starts them. She meditates twice per day once in the mornings and once in the evenings.

Next we'll talk about the business rituals of three highly successful individuals. Number one a monsignor Ortega. He made it to the Forbes billionaire list as the second wealthiest person in the world. A Monsignor Ortega has five business rituals which have guided him to success one speed is very important. A monster Ortega took the retail industry by storm in 1975 when he founded his company named Zara. He used the tactic of ensuring that two times per week his store was restocked with the latest fashion. Another one of his strategies was getting new styles of clothing before his competitors and the timely processing of customers orders.

Within 48 hours a monsignor Ortega's plan worked because he was able to satisfy his market better than his competitors and have earned his organization the name of fast fashion to be obsessed with your customers' needs. One of a monsignor Ortega's mottos is that the clients are the driving force behind a business and should always be the central focus when designing your business customers needs must also be your focal point when you are deciding on the operational systems that you will implement at your business style of clothing that you will be selling and any other activity that requires you interacting with your customers.

Being customer focused meant that a monster Ortega conducted consistent market research; his detailed analysis included him observing fashion blogs and directly garnering information from customers to keep a brief of the current trends in clothing. 3 being in control of your distribution channels. Monsignor Ortega capitalizes on the cost effectiveness of china clothing. But he also imports most of his products from other regions such as Morocco, Spain and Portugal. Designing and selling his products is one medium of how a monsignor Ortega swiftly meets the needs of his market by supplying them with the latest trends in fashion. He also utilizes a local network of sewing shops by having his designs cut and treated in mills.

Then they are sewn by local sewing shops for being committed to your roots. His ears buzzing from the ideas his employees share with him as he sits and works alongside them is the only office that a monsignor Ortega has ever had. A monsignor Ortega is from humble beginnings. He is the son of a housemaid and railway worker but his desire for a better life led him to stop attending school at the age of 14 to start earning. Knowing what it's like to have nothing. A monster, Ortega never got himself in office but instead he takes a hands-on approach by working with his employees.

Age has not slowed him down because even at the age of 80 a monsignor Ortega still goes to his office. On most days five continuous innovations complacency has no place among those who want to progress. And for those who want to remain successful, to become complacent is the biggest mistake you can make. You must have either a grow or die attitude and if you really want to be innovative then you cannot focus on the results. Number two. Carlos Slim Hello. Carlos Slim Helu has the tag of the fourth richest man in the world according to the Forbes billionaire list. He has 10 business rituals, one making money in a downturn. Recessions cannot hinder Carlos Slim Helu from acquiring new businesses.

His strategy is to take advantage of the companies that have been affected by the economic crisis which have no significant financial problems. Some of the best companies are sold for half their values during a recession. Carlos Slim Helu was able to purchase the largest cement company in the world. See Max during the recession. See Max currently has a net worth of approximately 6 billion thanks to simplicity in organizational structures. His best having a simple organizational structure with minimal hierarchical levels will allow executives to lower line employees to be able to interact more frequently, sustain flexibility and assist in quick decision making capability.

3 remain focused on innovation, growth training and quality. It is vital that you focus on innovation, growth quality of products, training for employees and continually improving production processes to analyze your organization based on global benchmarks. Seek the most cost effective means when possible to reduce expenses and increase productivity as well as your competitiveness for you must live without fear and guilt. Carlos Slim Hello believes fear is the worst weakness that men can have. Fear first weakens you then it impedes your action and eventually leads to depression.

He believes that guilt is a terrible burden in people's lives which influences the way one thinks and acts guilt and fear create difficulty for your present day and it's a hindrance for your future to overcome both fear and guilt. One must have good sense except ourselves as we are which means with whatever virtue disappointments and realities. 5 making wise investments in areas that customers find it difficult to avoid you. Carlos Slim Helu has made investments in a variety of industries. He has invested in the health sector, clothing industry, real estate bakeries, telecommunication academic institutions and museums just to name a few.

Carlos Slim who lost many investments have given him the opportunity to serve his customers daily through various mediums making it impossible for them to conduct business and not contribute to one of his establishments. 6 A good education will assist you to manage a big business better. Carlos Slim Helu believes that good decision making facilitates business success. You'll be able to make better business decisions if you are armed with the information to do so. This comes from increasing your knowledge through education. 7. Try to be humble no matter your status. Carlos Slim Helu is aware that riches also come with a lot of responsibility. However this has not prevented him from spending time with his family.

He assigned two days out of each week for quality time with his family. One day for dinner with his sons and another day for dinner with his twenty three grandchildren Carlos Slim Helu with all his billions still drives himself to work which is approximately an hour away from his home. He also lived in the same home in the same neighborhood for over 40 years. Prepare yourself for big opportunities Carlos Slim Helu believes one of the characteristics of becoming a successful entrepreneur is having the skill to identify great business opportunities and capitalize on your chances. Nine committing to the game entrepreneurship and investing is like a game.

If you want to succeed then it requires you to become committed to your entrepreneurial process and make decisions as if you are playing to win your entrepreneur and investing game to achieve success. Then comprehending your business to the core allegedly. Carlos Slim Helu controls approximately 200 companies in different regions around the globe. He was able to accomplish this by ensuring that he comprehends his business to the core. David Coke the 10th billionaire on the Forbes billionaires list David Coke shared his five tips for you to start learning from those who are rich, one creating wealth through earnings and not saving successful individuals like David Coke have continuous thoughts on how to earn big money and how to expand their potential profits.

If you are not significantly increasing the sum of money that you have then there is a good chance that your savings will not make you a wealthy person to never be afraid to believe in your ability and you should take smart risks. Many individuals refuse from taking risks because the possibility exists that they might fail. However those who are successful know that you have to take risks both financially and in your personal life. If you want to earn significant rewards, successful individuals also accept that failure is the price you pay for your ultimate learning experiences and you must develop the confidence to continue after you have failed. 3 Do not become emotionally attached to money-prospering individuals.

Take a rational approach when they are building their wealth. They do not allow any negative emotions like anxiety, greed or regret to daunt their financial decisions which have led to better chances for them to become successful to capitalize on all your opportunities as successful individuals. Understand that every opportunity presents the possibility for them to achieve more.

Even if it's a partnership project or they are just negotiating to venture into a new business they understand as well as appreciate the significance of networking. Successful individuals are always seeking new business ventures while capitalizing on their current assets to generate more income from different areas. Their positive attitude in every opportunity contributes to achievements in their business ventures and also to their wealth.

5.

Understanding that your time does not equal money dispel the belief that the time you spent working hard will be equivalent to your level of success. Undoubtedly successful individuals do work hard but they have to work even smarter. It's not necessarily how hard you work but how smart you are. Smart working means you strategize your time wisely and how you utilize your assets for them to assist you to increase your earnings. You should aspire to become an expert in your field no matter what field of business you're working in. If your greatest desire is to disengage yourself from the grip of poverty then you should adopt the rituals of the wealthy. Be fearless and have absolute confidence in your abilities. Believe that you deserve to have all the best that life has to offer.

Empowering & Disempowering Rituals

In this chapter we'll talk about empowering and disempowering rituals. But before that take a moment to ask yourself are my rituals empowering me or are they disempowering me. Make a list of your daily rituals that you've been doing over the past 10 years. Analyze the outcome of each of these rituals from your analysis of the habits that you have developed over the time. How did they assist you in progressing to your desired goals? How has your daily routine affected your relationship with your family and your friends? The answers to the above questions are ones which clearly state that your habits have generated only a negative or mostly negative impact in your life.

Then it is evident that you have disempowering rituals. It is time to change those disempowering rituals to empowering rituals. Next we'll talk about the power of your thoughts. Did you know that you have the power to change your thoughts which will eventually influence your actions. Every one of your actions came about because of a thought that you had initiated. Whether the idea came about consciously or it was a subconscious thought therefore to create empowering rituals. You will have to learn how to reprogram your mind to accomplish the reprogramming of your thoughts. You first have to find an empowering ritual that you will be using to replace the disempowering one.

Start your day with the right attitude full of energy and refreshed with ideas. When your day gets off to a good start you will be able to use your time more productively. We all have the same 24 hours in a day but how we structure our activities for the day can make a lot of difference. Let's take a look at some disempowering rituals that you might be practicing and we're not aware that they are not empowering you nine common disempowering rituals one getting out of bed long after the sun has comfortably settled itself in the sky and has provided great warmth for the Earth to lack of physical and mental exercise three unhealthy eating habits which are leading to degenerative and other fatal health issues for your time is used for reading and watching the wrong kind of materials which cannot assist you to achieve your ultimate goals 5 the individuals that we interact with on a daily basis influence our thought process a lot more than we often realize.

Evaluate your acquaintances if you associate yourself with people who are thriving for success or who are already successful then you will be motivated to change your lifestyle to be more in line with the successful people whom you are now associating yourself with. 6 Never make any plans for your day, you just go with the flow of any events. If you are not making plans to achieve then you have quickly set yourself up for failure. So do not be surprised when you reap failures resulting in seven poor time management. You might have made plans for your day but you spend too much time conducting rituals that are unproductive eight.

While it is true that most of the world's wealthiest individuals might not have a master's degree, they continually educate themselves through daily reading of books or by watching various chapters that will assist them in improving their skill sets. The poor allocation of your finances is a disempowering ritual. Investing your money in things that cannot return a profit on your dollar will not let you become rich. It is nice to have a fancy car, beautiful clothes and dine at the best restaurants. But these must only be a reward for the assets you have amassed through your hard work living like the rich and famous.

When your bank account along with your wallet is still living in poor man's land is a perfect example of you allocating your funds poorly. All the finer things of life that you want to enjoy will still be available when you have mastered your success rituals and you are financially capable of living life as a wealthy and famous individual. Next we'll move on to talk about six empowering rituals: one exercise your greatest wealth will always be your health. You should never sacrifice your health to achieve wealth. Your wealth will never truly restore your health and you might not even live long enough to enjoy your success too.

You must eat healthy and ensure you have adequate rest. To get up early in the mornings a great ritual that you must develop is to get out of bed early in the mornings creating a great head start to your day and life begins with you getting up early to make plans in your journal for the following day. Before you go to bed at night and evaluate activities of your day 5, find time to unwind and meditate and spend some quality time with those you love. 6. Investing yourself by increasing your knowledge about the field that you are in and also learn how to spend your money wisely consistently assess how your current assets can be allocated to allow you to earn more in different areas.

What you do daily influences your life. If your rituals are disempowering then you will never yield positive or favorable results. On the contrary if your rituals are empowering then you have a greater possibility of achieving some form of reward success starts in your mind with the thoughts that are in the forefront of your head because those thoughts are what will eventually empower your daily actions take a bit of advice from a woman who has dragged herself from the gutter of poverty to stand proudly among the wealthy. Oprah Winfrey stated what we dwell on is who we become.

Building Your Own Success Rituals

In this chapter we'll discover how to build your own success rituals. You cannot build your own success rituals if you are not aware of what it is that you need to be doing to ensure you become successful in your given field. Want to be successful, if you actually want to become successful, then you must find out what rituals those who are successful in your given field have. Based on the information that you have gathered, you will build your own success rituals. I believe it can be comfortably said that the majority of successful individuals are always out of bed before the sun rises. With that said the first ritual that you should build is ensuring that you are also out of bed before the sun rises. Let's examine the benefits of rising early in the mornings.

1 There's just something about the dawn of a new day before the sun makes its appearance in the sky that fills your inner vessel with a lot of hope. Not even the polluted air which is often found in urban regions can eradicate that morning whiff of hope. Even if you just open a window in your home and take a swift deep breath of it, a second benefit of rising early in the mornings is that you don't have a lethargic feeling which typically comes with rising after the sun has risen. 3 You can get a lot more done during the day by having an early start. For the peacefulness of the morning gives you a chance to filter your thoughts more accurately and make better plans.

So you have mastered the task of getting up early. That's great. However you must use your time productively. The best part of becoming wealthy is to know that you had done so while maintaining or with no compromise to your health to maintain or not to compromise your health. You will have to watch what you consume and ensure that you do at least a half hour of physical exercise each day or for a minimum of three days per week. Did you know that the most successful individuals have incorporated exercise into their daily routine. Therefore the next morning ritual that you should develop is exercise exercises important to get your body in shape but it also helps with the Vel upping a healthier mind for you to function better exercising as you know is only a part of the process to keep healthy.

You also have to eat healthy if you want the exercise to work efficiently. Exercising and eating healthy is one way that you might cheat death to live a little longer so you can enjoy your wealth. So I'm sure it's worth taking the shot and having a healthy lifestyle. Besides that, the aspiration to become the best at what you do is something that you must take into consideration when you are building your rituals. The great inventor and co-founder of Apple Steve Jobs said innovation distinguishes between a leader and a follower. You should consistently brainstorm for ideas that will improve the plans you already have and what will uniquely set you apart from others. Whoever is the best in the market will also amass the most success.

Allocate time to cover all areas of your life. You will need to find the time to exercise, meditate , make your schedule and for work you need time to have fun with your family and friends. Start creating your own opportunities for success by ensuring you have some highly successful individuals in your circle. You already know that success is something that you have to work to obtain. So you not only have to think like those who are the best but start talking, dressing and acting like you are the best too. That's a sure way of setting yourself up to become the best in your given field.

6 Core Success Rituals

In this chapter we'll talk about the six core success rituals before that. There's one thing that you have to keep in mind. Each area is important to create balance in your life. If you ignore one of the six core areas of success then you will not be able to function at your best. You will have a sense of lacking in your life and you might even waste your time trying to fill the void with the wrong things. Now let's look into the six core areas of success. One physical health two emotions three relationships for career or business five finances six spirituality one physical health the emphasis can never be too much on how important it is to ensure you do all that's possible to sustain your physical health.

It's quite logical that one of two things will occur if you do not maintain your physical health. It's either that you will have to spend your fortune on medications and doctors or you will be snatched to an early death due to some form of health issue. Exercise, eating healthy, getting adequate sleep and drinking a lot of water can assist in keeping you healthy. Two emotions affect your mind. If you are mentally unhealthy or unstable then you cannot make objective decisions. A decision that is made when someone is emotionally unstable can wreak havoc on your life and has the potential to become very drastic which we have all either heard, read or experienced personally all the six core areas of success are correlated.

Take for example if something happens to trigger your emotions in a negative way. If you're feeling sad or you might be angry you can always exercise to calm yourself down. It's not only your negative emotions that you need to learn to control because if you are too excited or happy but you can also make a wrong decision. For example if you are overzealous you might spend money on things which you don't need and that money could have been invested in something that will increase your income. Life is about creating the right balance in everything you do. Three relationships can affect your health and your emotions.

A toxic relationship will leave you with feelings of despair and anger, unhappiness and rage can lead to depression. Depression will affect your progress either by you losing time to work or by you making decisions which will ultimately result in failure. The benefit of good relationships will create heaven for you on Earth. The world in your eyes is at peace because your heart is full of love and your mind will have its cover made from thoughts of joy. You will function better. You will be more eager to get up in the mornings because you are grateful for another day to be with the ones you love. Examine your relationships and see how they are impacting your life.

If being around someone makes you feel burdened or you feel as if that person is pulling all your hope and the joy out of you then that is a toxic connection. You need to disconnect from that person. Relationships that motivate you to become better or the ones that help your ideas sparkle are what you need in your life. For career or business, did you know that simply by observing the attitude people display at their place of work can always tell you who loves their job from those who don't. If you are not in the job or business which makes you feel that this is what you were born to do then you might be in the wrong field.

Your career or business must leave you feeling fulfilled no matter the obstacles you face daily.

The belief that the world could not exist without you doing that business or career finds its resting place in your mind and heart went in the right field. It will be easier to keep focus and because of the passion you have for your career and business failure can not convince you to quit. 5 finances, wealth and happiness is all of our hearts desire. However if you want to be wealthy it might take years of hard work to become rich but it only takes a minute with a bad investment which will result in you losing all your money. Never spend money on things just because you want to impress others. That is definitely not a ritual of success. Individuals and the wealthiest people live humble lives. You must also adopt the principle of giving back to the less fortunate.

Just this how you will start practicing the other success rituals. This is one habit. You must also allocate whatever you can afford to charity now and as your wealth increases then you increase the portion for charity as well. 6 spirituality no matter what your religion preference may be. Spirituality is an important aspect of spiritual success. Spirituality can be found all around you from the time you spend in nature to meditation to your religious practices. Did you know that spirituality has the ability to ground you and keep you close to both your own personal feelings and help you work through anxiety and emotion which will enable you to make sound and important judgments, choose a spiritual ritual for yourself and stick with it. Each and every day.

Morning Success Rituals

In this chapter we'll talk about the morning success rituals. A vast amount of information was shared about morning success rituals throughout these chapters. And it's evident that you have to start your day right to create the perfect momentum for the rest of the day. One smile. Your first exercise routine should be a smile. A smile is free. It's the best cosmetic surgery. And it will help to relax you. Try smiling right now and see if you don't feel an instant peace in your heart. To show gratitude after you smile then you should show gratitude to the world around you for the ability to experience a new day through meditation. You will hear your inner voice more distinctly.

You will have the opportunity to search your soul and discover your most profound desires. Sometimes if you listen keenly you will begin to understand exactly what your path should be. Three drink more water. Drink some water at least to hydrate your body. Water helps with circulation, improves your skin tone, assists with your weight loss and the purification of your body. Water is the best strength to have. It is imperative that you always consult your physician about things that will affect how your body functions before attempting to do them for positive affirmation.

You need positive affirmation motivational audios or books are a great source of motivation. After you meditate then you can listen or read something from your favorite motivator. Positive affirmation is a must among your daily routine and you have to learn to be your greatest source of inspiration. This will help to block all the negative voices which will tell you that you do not have the ability to achieve feeding your mind with positive food sets the tone for you to improve your knowledge. Take some time in the morning to read most of the knowledge you will acquire in life will come from your experiences and what you teach yourself. 5.

Exercise. Next you engage in some vigorous exercise. Go for a long walk or run, do some stretches or yoga. Get physically active. By the time you've completed the above activities you will feel fully rejuvenated and ready to face the new day. You can start with your most challenging task and then work your way through the others. How you and your day can impact how your day starts. Therefore aim to end your day on a good note. Your body needs time to unwind from the wear and tear of the work day. Take some time to relax in the evenings and designate time for your family.

Never neglect the ones you love in pursuit of your wealth. It will be very lonely at the top of the ladder of success if you do not have anyone to share your success with. Plan for tomorrow. Make plans for the next day. Prioritize your task. Make a list of those that are critical to least important. Assess your day if you have accomplished your entire task and if you have not what prevented you from achieving that task. If it is possible you should exercise in the evenings to say goodbye to the world of work with whatever relaxation techniques you have and settle in for a healthy prosperous future.

Evening Success Rituals

In this chapter I will share with you the evening's success rituals for going to bed every night feeling fulfilled with a big smile on your face. These rituals are the follow up to your morning rituals to reflect and celebrate after your day's activities. While mourning rituals are highly encouraged to be incorporated into everyone's daily routine, the evening rituals are equally important to get the most out of your day. After all there's no point to start off a race full of energy but no idea how to end it. So I don't want you to miss this crucial part to inspire your success and celebrate it.

You may be consistently crushing your goals one after another but unless you take the time to celebrate every victory in your life then you're definitely not getting the most out of your day and missing out on a lot of magic moments and sense of fulfillment that you should be experiencing at this moment. Here are the evening success rituals that I highly recommend incorporating into your evening routine. 1 empowering evening questions to seize your magic moments. 3. CELEBRATE ONE empowering evening questions at the beginning of the evening success rituals. The main focus is to reflect on your day and the best way to reflect is to ask powerful questions, not just any questions that beat yourself up.

I call these powerful questions empowering evening questions designed to help you reflect on your entire day and come up with constructive ideas to shape a better tomorrow. So the first thing you should do is to find a quiet place where you won't be easily disturbed and distracted for a set amount of time in order to go deep into your daily reflection. Did you know the questions you asked? Determine what you focus on. That's the reason why the type of questions you ask yourself is extremely important. Ask a lousy question and you'll feel lousy. Ask a good question and you will feel amazing. The fact is there's always good and bad in each day and what you ask yourself decides what you'll focus on each night before hitting the sack.

What you focus on determines how you feel about that particular day. Since there's always good and bad, why not be proactive and decide that you only want to acknowledge the good that happened that day. Since you can decide how you're going to feel at the end of the day, why not choose to feel good instead of bad. Guess what happens if you constantly ask yourself empowering evening questions every day will be an awesome day for you and you'll always feel like a rock star. Now think of the level of accomplishments, productivity and fulfillment you'll experience every day. I'll let you know about mine. Phenomenal. In fact there is no such thing as a bad day. It all starts with your focus and needs empowering. Evening questions will help you do just that.

Here's a list of questions that you can ask yourself every evening. What was fantastic about today. What did I learn today? What am I grateful for today? What was my biggest accomplishment for today? What would make today Great. Don't just write down all your answers. Try to feel the emotions and energy coursing through your veins as you read out your answers out loud. Do this with Level 10 intensity move gestures and smile wildly as you answer them. Allow yourself to feel proud, excited , happy , loved, appreciated etc. Trust me you'll be amazed by what this simple exercise can do to your physical and emotional well-being.

The more juice you'll get from the empowering evening questions exercise to seizing your magic moments after you've gone through the empowering evening questions exercise you'll be in an incredible state but you don't want to stop right there. You should take this opportunity to seize these emotions and feelings by journaling all your successes, accomplishments and magic moments. Otherwise they'd be forgotten. So take out a journal and write down everything that happened on that day, Miss down everything you had done and all the powerful moments that you want to remember later on. Time passes by so fast and we easily forget to really take in and appreciate the little things at the end of your life.

You won't be able to remember everything but only certain moments. So I want to encourage you to take your time and capture all your successes and Magic Moments into your journal one day when you're feeling down and you see no hope in life you have a journal to go back to and remind yourself of all the magic moments that you once had and realize that your life is actually more incredible than you think. By journaling your magic moments you'll be aware of what you were doing with your time and celebrate your victory 3 celebrate. Last but not least, celebrate your day to your heart's content. You deserve it. This is a powerful way to positively reinforce yourself.

Don't beat yourself up for things you didn't do, tasks you procrastinated, food you shouldn't need etc. because that's what most people do. Which prompts them to feel awful and guilty about themselves to make things worse. They repeat this process every day and they end up in a downward spiral that sets themselves up for more failures. Why bring so much pain in your life when there are so many good things that happen every day. Why not start recognizing and celebrating all the good that happened that day. What gets rewarded gets repeated. Did you know that when you celebrate your victory often you'll invite more amazing things into your life.

And soon you'll be conditioned to notice the good in every little thing that happens in your life. And soon you'll develop powerful habits such as gratitude, consistency , tenacity and self-discipline. So how do you celebrate? You really don't have to complicate things. Celebrating means giving yourself pleasure. It could be as simple as patting yourself on the back and saying to yourself. Good job or treat yourself to a whole hearty meal giving thanks. Listening to your favorite music or meditating with gratitude the key is to give yourself pleasure. Oftentimes we wait for others to praise, acknowledge and reward us in order to feel happy, appreciated and fulfilled. Why not be proactive and reward yourself when you can choose to be happy. Right now.

Conclusion

Do not give up on your dreams. It might take time for you to achieve your goals but with the power that is embedded in your mind you can conquer the world. One day at a time. Never let procrastination cripple your progress. Do not let failure deter you. Learn whatever chapter that comes with failing. Then restart your journey. The more you use your skills you will discover other hidden treasures of ability that were buried in you. I can guarantee that you will be astonished at the things you can do. Your talent can take you to places you have not even started to imagine. The hard work and sacrifices you make to attain success will be worth it. In fact when you start your journey to success each challenge you overcome will become a distant memory because the rewards will outweigh the struggles. Remember success is a lifestyle one that a taste of it is very addictive.

You can have your taste of success too. I might not know your name or where you're from. I might not know what you've been through or what you're going through now. However I know that you have something within you something that sets you apart from the rest of the individuals in your line of work. You need to find that part of your skill because it is your key to the door of success. No one in the world can do it for you. This is something you have to do on your own. I believe the fact that you have purchased this chapter is because that key which is part of your skill has been nudging you. It is telling you that you can do this. You have what it takes. Do not be afraid.

All it takes are some small steps and the small steps will one day be a very long journey, a journey of no regrets because you tried and had achieved everything in life as a choice. The only thing we do not have a choice about is when we will die. Watch your inner thoughts. They will influence what you do and speak positive words to yourself every day. You will have many options but never choose to quit no matter how bad things get. Working on your self education is a powerful tool. Utilizing technology makes some connections with people who are successful in your field. Sell them your plans and describe your goals with such passion that they have to listen to you. Prepare yourself for the nose. It's just part of your learning experience on your journey. Do not get mad at those who will reject your plans.

You cannot blame them for not understanding the greatness that lies within you. Most of the individuals who will tell you no now will one day plead with you to join their team to keep a firm hold on your spirituality. It can ground you, bring you clarity and motivate you to understand your inner self. Finding your place in the universe and with spirituality does not need to be religious based. Spirituality is a state of conscience that enables you to specify your desires and future with a clear mind and relaxed body. So what will be your choice I believe you will take your first small step to success by conquering your fear and misery because you are going to build your own success rituals as soon as you finish watching this chapter thank you for watching this chapter and I am looking forward to seeing you at the top of the ladder of success. Good luck.

www.ingramcontent.com/pod-product-compliance
Lightning Source LLC
Chambersburg PA
CBHW072006210526
45479CB00003B/1081